Red Beard the Pirate

Written by Lisa Thompson

Pictures by Craig Smith and Lew Keilar

Stanley is the captain on a pirate ship.

Everyone calls him Captain Red Beard.

3

The pirate ship is called The Black Beast.
The Black Beast has a very colorful crew.

Loud Lizzie is first mate. Bones, the sea
dog, is in charge of the lookout. Fingers, the
parrot, keeps her eyes on the treasure maps.

Captain Red Beard loves sailing the high seas.

He likes it when the seas are big and rough.

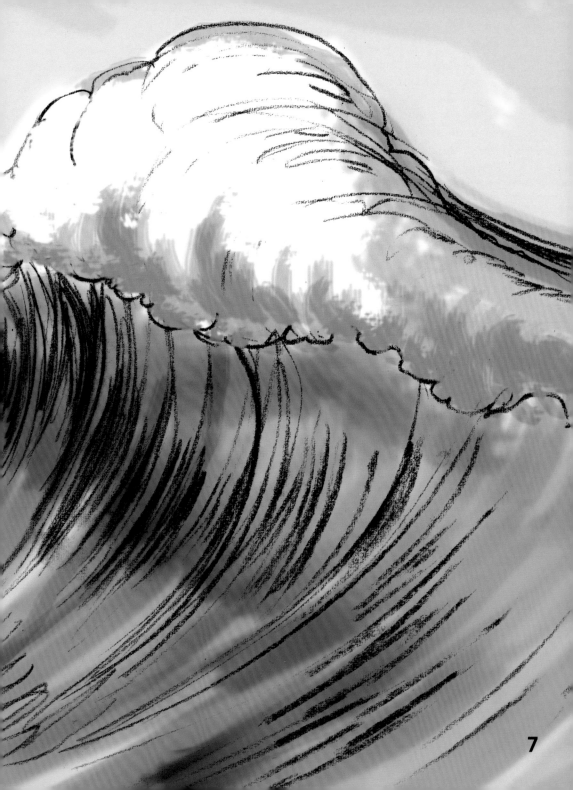

Captain Red Beard loves meeting other pirates.

They are not always pleased to see him.

Captain Red Beard loves giving orders.

"Scrub the decks! Mend those sails!
Get me my parrot! Tighten the rigging!"

His crew often has better things to do.

Captain Red Beard loves swinging in his hammock, singing pirate songs.

He does not sing at all well.

13

Captain Red Beard loves swapping pirate stories over dinner, while he shines his pirate boots.

Captain Red Beard loves his pirate sneer and making up new pirate sayings.

"Arrrhhh! You're a gold nugget short of an empty booty!"

"Flying cannonballs!"

Captain Red Beard loves shooting the cannons and flying his pirate flag.

Do you know what Captain Red Beard loves most of all?

He loves finding treasure.

The Black Beast sails and sails and sails. The crew sails night and day, day and night. Captain Red Beard needs to learn how to read a map.

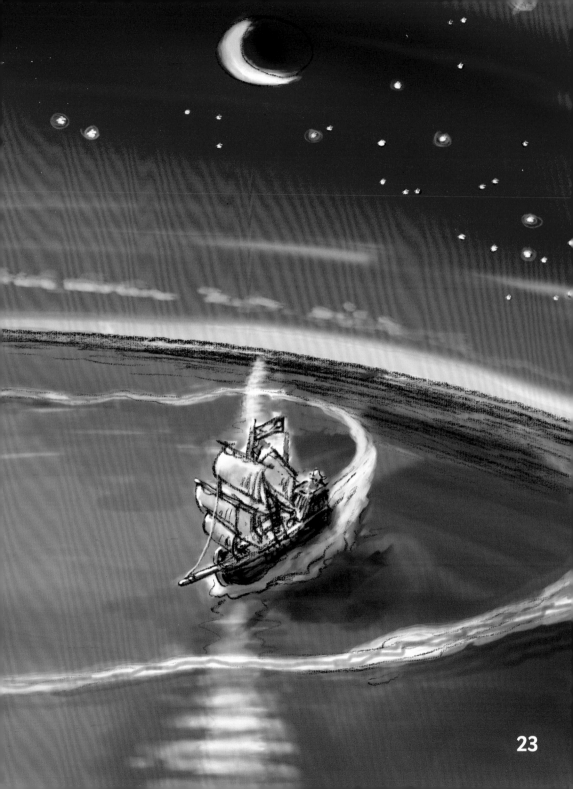